MEDICINE WHEEL OF MY RECOVERY

MEDICINE WHEEL OF MY RECOVERY

MICKEY M.

authorHOUSE®

AuthorHouse™
1663 Liberty Drive
Bloomington, IN 47403
www.authorhouse.com
Phone: 1-800-839-8640

Published by AuthorHouse   12/10/2012

ISBN: 978-1-4772-9842-8 (sc)
ISBN: 978-1-4772-9841-1 (e)

Library of Congress Control Number: 2012923402

Introduction

Hello, my name is Mickey (Three River), and with the help of the Father Spirit, the creator, I am a grateful recovering addict/alcoholic.

I call myself an addict/alcoholic because that's just what I am. I know there are recovery programs out there that swear up and down that there is no such thing as a recovering addict/alcoholic. They say either you're an addict or alcoholic but you can't be both. Maybe so, but somewhere down the line I screwed up because I know fact well that if I had a drink, the first thing I would look for is some drugs. And if I took drugs, the first thing I would do is look for alcohol. If I couldn't get both, then I wouldn't get the high I was looking for. The balance of both chemicals was my daily choice of drugs.

This program eliminates the person you imitate when you're drinking or taking and leaves you with that wonderful human being you left behind. A place where you become a miracle and a messenger for those who are still out there suffering by showing them that it can be done. I say miracle because it takes a miracle to stop us from drinking and taking, and miracles only come from one place. May you find him now. For years, I tried to stop drinking and taking, but I just could not do it so I gave up, and I have not had a drink or drugs since. That was twenty-six years ago. So many people have asked me how I stayed sober so long. I have to admit to them, I didn't. Only a power greater than me can restore me to sanity.

No, I did not change my mind about quitting. I changed my direction about quitting. Convinced that I did not have what it takes to stop, I closed my eyes and said, "If there really is something out there, you're going to have to get me sober, cause I sure the hell can't do it." The very next morning, I found myself in an AA meeting full of weird people drinking coffee with nothing in it but cream and sugar, people smiling and laughing and yet, what I found interesting was everyone that spoke gave my deepest confession and experience. This is why, before long, I felt part of it. And this is what I been looking for, and been for twenty-six years

By relating the program to the Native American tradition, I have learned to find the balance of the four directions, and within my inner and outer spiritual self through the Big Book and the Twelve Steps. Finding the balance or my inner and outer spiritual self was one of the most important steps I have taken in the program. For example, the Twelve Steps can be related to medicine that the animal gives us. Like the totem pole of our inner spirit, which is the spiritual healing source for us, as the medicine from the totem pole of the Twelve Steps is to our sobriety.

Step 1— We admitted we were powerless over alcohol—that our lives had become unmanageable. This equals the medicine of the bear. The bear seeks sweet truth from the honey. The spiritual message from the bear is, "Without truth, there is no change."

Step 2— Came to believe that a power greater than ourselves could restore us to sanity. This equals the medicine of the deer. Teaches us that the strongest strength is softness. The spiritual message from the deer is "come to the Father Spirit weak and humble, and he'll give you strength."

Step 3— Made a decision to turn our will and our lives over to the care of Father Spirit, as we understand him. This equals the medicine of the horse. Is his power. The spiritual message from the horse is, "When you're weak, I will carry you."

Step 4— Made a searching and fearless moral inventory of ourselves. This equals the medicine of the fox. To be unseen and observant, the spiritual message from the fox is, "See yourself in your own mind's eye."

Step 5— Admitted to Father Spirit, to ourselves, and to another human being the exact nature of our wrongs. This equals the medicine of buffalo. Unity and harmony, the buffalo is the one that brought us the sacred pipe in two parts. The steam representing the male and the bowl representing the female together bring smoke in, which is the visual prayer . . .

Step 6— Were entirely ready to have Father Spirit remove all these defects of character. This equals the medicine of the owl. The night eagle, wisdom, the death of something whether it's bad or good.

Step 7— Humbly asked him to remove our shortcomings. This equals the medicine of a coyote, shortcoming, opening the same door expecting something different. Plays tricks on himself.

Step 8— Made a list of all persons we had harmed, and became willing to make amends to them all. This equals the medicine of the wolf, a loyal friend . . .

Step 9— Made direct amends to such people wherever possible, except when to do so would injure them or others. This equals the medicine of the mountain lion, courage . . .

Step 10— Continued to take personal inventory, and when we were wrong, promptly admitted it. This equals the medicine of the crow. Change, don't be afraid of change, nothing moves until it changes. Believe in yourself and stand in your truth . . .

Step 11— Sought through prayer and meditation to improve our conscious contact with Father Spirit, as we understood him. Praying only for knowledge of his will for us and the power to carry them out. This equals the medicine of the eagle. As your inner spirit soars high into the skies, let the warm breath of the Great Spirit's words under your wing keep you from falling . . .

Step 12— Had a spiritual awakening as the result of these steps. We tried to carry this message to alcoholics and to practice these principles in all our affairs. This equals the medicine of the hawk, the messenger . . .

Brothers and sisters, keep in your hearts that man finds destiny; destiny does not find man. This is why one does not get over recovery; one goes through recovery.

When the tears fall from one's heart, not from the eyes, do they know the cries of an alcoholic because much more has been lost than the eyes can see?

When in troubled mind, give it to the west of the four directions, where the skies meets the land and the Grandfather Sun lies to rest, that the Grandfather Sun can take it down with him as the day ends. Then wait for a new beginning from the east. While you wait, seek the three sister stars in the skies that bring you the three messages of wisdom: believe, trust, and faith.

Face the morning star and hear from your heart the wisdom it brings that tells you always to be in the day given, not in the day past. Then with a new beginning in the morning light receive your conditions back as tools for the day . . .

I came into a program recovery looking for a new life, because drugs and alcohol no longer corrected the world I accepted as reality, and I wanted to know what I was doing when I was doing it. Where we are today mentally is because of our choices or the results of our choice, and everything we do is because of our choices or the results of our choices. What the recovering program does is turn our destructive choices we made in the past into constructive decision for today. We learn to have a deeper yes, when we say yes, and a deeper no, when we say no, as we learn in seeking the Father Spirit's will for us. What is Father Spirit's will? Father Spirit's will is the meaning of life for us, which is to be the best we can possibly be in all we do in sobriety. This can be accomplished if you allow it to. People in the program of recovery can be the best they can be if they give themselves permission to. Once again, the choice is yours.

Let's talk a little more on Father Spirit's will. The creature's will will never put you so far from him that he won't be able to reach out and give you strength. This is why the human spirit is stronger than anything that can happen to it. Never underestimate the power of your spiritual self. Nothing can overpower you; you just think it has. Remember your spiritual self is strong enough to go on after you die. In working or even trying to work on the Father Spirit's will, you're never alone. You find the Father Spirit's will through the strength of your spiritual belief. How do you get a spiritual belief? The Twelve Steps of recovery. When working on Father Spirit's will, we are in the process of our lives; accept it that way. Don't accept everything that goes wrong as a punishment instead of a lesson taught. We just haven't made it a lesson learned yet. Your wrongs are just as important as your rights when you use your wrongs as a tool. Sometimes people misinterpret their situation; it's all in the matter of acceptance. Your acceptance is what you live in today. Let's not forget your belief is your reality, and a dream is a fantasy. Believe in it and make it a reality. Give all your situation time to form into a complete result before you judge it. Keep in mind patience is not our best friend. The best medicine is having to learn what we have to learn in order for us to recognize and appreciate our destination when we get there. What I'm saying here is don't finalize the miracle before it's finished or you will be living in an incomplete miracle. That would be like eating fruit before it's ripe. In this program, I learned to respect myself as somebody. When I was out there drinking and using, I was just anybody. With the help of this program, I am no longer surviving. I am a survivor today. I like to think positive of myself. Why not? I deserve it.

For example, after taking step 1, I no longer called myself the problem but the solution. Solution works with problems, but problems do not work with problems. The blind leading the blind.

I learned to believe in myself and have faith in what I do. As long as I believe, I will never be alone, and as long as I have faith, I will always have a conscious power greater than myself of my understanding. In which I choose to call "Father Spirit." I ask my conscious power greater than myself for help in making daily decisions. He in turn gives me wisdom for my daily direction, and that's because he knows I have an alcoholic mind and I tend to be more concerned of what is going on in front of me instead of what is going on inside me. The hardest part of this program for me was my own resistance and that is because I was more afraid of what I did not know than what I did know. I kept going in circles and life kept slipping right by me. The circle I'm talking about is the one people get stuck in when they start drinking and using by repeating themselves over and over again. Like opening the same door over and over expecting something different on the other side. The circle of life that gets smaller and smaller as one continues drinking and using. They get high, spend their whole paycheck, fight with their spouses, become smart-alecks with all their friends, and so on. Then when it's all over and you made a mess of things, you apologize to your spouse and friends, put the house back together again, and now the frosting on the cake: swear you will never do it again. Then when all is well and back in order again, the alcoholic accepts the positive reconstructed life as a validation to get drunk again. This time, of course, with a little more control on the drinking and using, like maybe less beer and whiskey, or less whiskey and more beer. The alcoholic mind tells you that someone does not like me so my whole week would be shot. Could this attitude behavior mean something? Then too, I always have the temptation of turning thoughts into snowballs and rolling them down a snowy hillside, making them bigger and bigger than what I started with. I know I have the disease because to this day you're able to correct and control the issue next time. But they repeat the same issue again with the wife, friends, paycheck, and so on. Except this time around, they get themselves a good old DUI, or as in today it's a DWI, and lose their license. So next time around, their circle gets smaller, because this time around they don't have license in their circle. Next time they lose their spouse in which their circle or course gets even smaller. Then their friends, job, home, etc. Now their circle of life is so small it becomes like one foot nailed down to the ground and the other foot going in a circles. Then they do the brilliant and end up in jail for a while. So their circle of life is so small it looks like a spot. This is what we call a tight spot. The program of AA is to help us get out of that circle and into a spiral of life so that we can get somewhere in life before it's too late.

Let no one tell you that it's never to late. Tell them to go to a cemetery and say that. Remember this: neither time nor tide waits for man.

Step one: we admitted we were powerless over alcohol, that our lives have become unmanageable. You never find anything in life until you find *self*.

Step two: come to believe that a power greater than ourselves could restore us to sanity. You never start healing until the pain is gone.

No matter how long I am in the program, I still have to keep on top of the disease. I have to for the rest of my life. With that in mind, I made awareness part of my daily life. I have to keep reminding myself to work only on self and not on issue. I forget that part of this disease comes from the codependency family, which tells me to fix everything but me. If I do anything to try to fix anyone, I am trying to take the Father Spirit's place in his or her life. That is why in these meetings we share, not teach. The listener is the only one that can turn sharing into teaching.

When I first came into this program, I did not believe people when they said they had fifteen or twenty years sobriety and say they still have the disease we talk about in recovery. Yet today after twenty-seven years clean and sober, the symptoms are still there. I'm still powerless over my reactions, but I notice the longer I stay in the program, the easier it is to deal with my reactions, and the stronger my program and the quicker I catch my reactions before they turn into actions. Even today when I'm at a party I can have twenty good friends and I find out my reactions suggest working on the problem before working on myself first so that I can express action from my reaction. Then I ask myself why does talking about myself feel like a confession? Today I am a believer that this disease will be with me until I die, so I try to keep awareness with me at all times.

In twenty-seven years, the only thing difference in this disease today is the stage I put it in, from practicing to recovering. This disease is a lot like cancer: you have it for life. You go to a doctor and get treatments for cancer to stabilize it, but the disease you go to meetings to stabilize it. The difference between cancer and the disease of alcohol and drugs is cancer will kill you at the end, and the disease will help you kill yourself at the end. As long as I have a good strong healthy program, I will never be a puppet of the world or for the disease again.

Sobriety is being happy, joyous, and free. Some people never see the results of their sobriety because they're too busy trying to get there, or they miss it because they think they already have it, just as I did. Like anyone else, I got on cloud nine and thought I had it. I was under the impression that after four or five weeks I was happy, joyous, and free. Instead, I was on cloud nine for over a year before I slowed my pace down to happy, joyous, and free, which is okay, just know where you're at in this state. In this program, we have to stop and take an inventory and see where we're at, as in step four and ten in the Twelve Steps of recovery. In addition, I become a listener of myself as well as others. It's not what they're sharing but what I hear. This tells me what I need to know. In other words, it's what we say in our minds and how we say it to ourselves that determines the quality of the output your mind will produce when you ask yourself a question. Whatever level you focus on is the level of answer you will receive. Ask yourself a dumb question; get yourself a dumb answer kind of thing. A person only hears what he is ready for from where he is at in the program. This is why the listener is the only one that can turn sharing 180 degrees into teaching.

In my early days in the program, I was advised of four medicine wheels in the program, Big Book,

Twelve Steps, meetings, and sponsorship. The reason for this is the Big Book you learn about the disease, the Twelve Steps you learn about yourself. Put them together and you learn about the alcoholic. Sponsor and meetings, meetings you learn to use tools, and your sponsor is your blueprint, and you put all those together. The alcoholic learns to build himself a house of life with it all.

When I first come into the program, all I wanted to talk about is everything that bothered me. This is a good thing because one has to let everything out and not hold anything in so we can make room for our freedom. Most old timers will not do that. Not that they're any different. It is just that the old timer deals with it differently. That is what we do in this program: learn to accept things differently. It's still there; the disease never changes just because you moved the disease from practicing to recovering. Nothing changes in the world or the disease, only in our days, and we do that through acceptance on daily basis with what we have gathered in these meetings.

Newcomers, through experience I say to you, give the program your best not your expectations.

The first thing I worked on in this program is learning to live without that drink. As my attitude progressed through this program, I worked on learning to live with the feeling of not having that drink. Keep in mind that craving is a feeling. The disease never changes. I just accept it different, as in step two of the Twelve Steps of recovery. I have to remember that drugs and alcohol were my parents. Every day you try, you're successful, because trying is success in process; it just is not complete yet. Be a successful person. Never stop working the program, and when fallbacks set in, let the rewards of attitude adjustment carry you. You don't have to be strong to work the program of recovery, just willing. Keep in mind the old Indian words from our ancestors: "The strongest strength is softness. Just tell yourself that you're worth it and deserve another chance. Love people for the returned energy. If you are capable of giving love, then you're capable of receiving love.

Don't let success be your anchor. Keep building with what you have already accomplished. As in step one to take step two, step one and two to take step three, step one, two, three, to take step four, and so on. It's called doing the best you can with what you got. Same goes for life. Use one success to help accomplish other successes. Success only stops when you do. The secret of success is *consistency.*

The disease of alcohol has a contract for you that reads, "Keep me active and I promise to do all your thinking for you." This contract is a sign when you take your next drink or drug. Then the contract goes on to say, "All the stories you heard in the AA meetings about events that happen because of alcohol thinking can rightfully be yours. To sign them, you just keep drinking and using and all those stories you hear in the meetings, and many, many more will truthfully be yours."

After you come into the program, you become an image. Use that image to communicate with others in helping others in bettering themselves. Teach them that whatever happens, let go. Let the Father Spirit have it. As we learn in surrender, surrendering is a spiritual way of communicating with yourself. Everything you go through in this program, bad and good, is just part of the process of getting you to become happy, joyous, and free, which we talk about in this book. Your only job is to navigate the situations so that we can learn and grow from them that we can help others that are in the same boat were in. The only time I receive problems is when I need to learn something, and that is because if I didn't need to learn something, I wouldn't be in that mental situation to begin with in the first place.

Sobriety is a miracle. Reach out and help someone who is trying to get there and become part of a miracle. Keep hanging around this program long enough, and eventually you will become part of it and it will be part of you. That's what keeps me here from the start. People started saying hi to me and getting to know them, then becoming friends and friends, is being *part of* . . . I find that it's no mistake me being here; there is no mistake in the creature's world, and so everything in this world is positive. You just have to look at it differently. Our mistakes are nothing but lessons. There is not a mistake that cannot be turned into a lesson. In this program, we just need to take a different direction than the one we have been taking. We have to go through the process of changing directions. That's all.

Many of the newcomers soon have a conscious power greater than them self shortly after they come into the program of recovery. They just don't recognize it. The Higher Power is the love you feel when you come into recovery. In which is your conscious power greater than yourself touching your heart. Please don't accept that as preaching because it's not. Today, I have a conscious power greater than myself of my understanding, and I choose to call him as my ancestors did, Father Spirit, and I know his will for me. He wants me to have a strong, loving, harmonious life. I know this because I trust and believe his will for me. The Father Spirit's will is something to know and not see; we furnish that. My conscious power greater than myself will not give me his will. I have to go out and get it through prayer and meditation, as it says in step eleven, "to carry that out." I have to activate Father Spirit's will. Instead of Father Spirit's will, I ask, "What can I do to help my Father Spirit's will for me?" My Father Spirit's will is like the Big Book. It's full of miracles, but you have to open it. Sometimes you pray and pray for a miracle and yet no answer. Many times, it's because it's our job in the first place to get it done. Know what your job is and what Father Spirit's job is. "The wisdom to know the difference." The closer you get to your conscious power greater than yourself, the easier the program becomes. In turn, no man is powerless with the strength of their conscious power greater than themselves.

Recovery is wrapped around two primary principles. First is self. Look at the Twelve Steps. Each step is directed to self. Read the Big Book. Each chapter is directed to self. Listen to the sharing in meetings. Everything said relates to self. Why? Because recovery is to help you to know yourself better. The more you know yourself, the better your attitude becomes. In turn, the better you're able to express yourself and the way you express yourself is not all in what you say but what you feel. As I mentioned before in step one, you never find anything in life until you find self first. Once you find self, you find roots. Nothing in the creator's world grows without roots. Not even a baby; the mother is the root. The root I am talking about is down in your gut where all the hate is. We have to nourish those roots with the program so they can grow upward into a beautiful smile, as it says in the promises of AA.

Now let us talk about the second primary principle, "The Program." The program is a place where one can identify by relating with others and becomes a third party of their life and identifies their behavior with spiritual reasons. For myself, I pictured AA meetings like a crystal ball where I can look into it and see my whole life inside of one little room. In doing so, I can get a better outlook of myself. Just like anything else, the better view you have of something, the better understanding you have of it and the easier it is to make changes. As a carpenter would look at the blueprints before he works on a house, you would before you work on a defect. The program is a room full of mirrors, sitting in chairs that you can be able to recognize yourself without any doubt through sharing and relating. The program is that way so you can find and start working on the original you. As a painter sands down to the original wood before he paints it or the paint will not last, neither will you. This is why self and program have to come together and become a team in order to reach sobriety.

The program became much easier to accept when I placed principle before personality in front of it because of all the different kind of people that sit in these meetings. However, keep in mind that AA needs you and other different beliefs and understanding in the same room to make it work. When newcomers come in these rooms and see the poor, the rich, Christian, spiritual, religious, they will receive their first message: the program is not prejudiced. This program has a reason for everybody who comes through the doors of a meeting. I may not know the reason and you may not know the reason, but the one next to me knows. Everyone in an AA meeting is an open door for another to relate to. That is why when you are sitting in a meeting, you are an encouragement to the people in the program. You just never know where the message is going to come from or where your message is going to go. The slogan, "Principles before personality," is another open door in receiving the message. You do not have to accept the individual's belief but you do have to respect the individual who stands by his belief. So if you have trouble with all of the above, please report to step four of the Twelve Steps of recovery.

There are three types of alcoholics, practicing and nonpracticing alcoholic. The only difference between those two is their breath, because they both think the same. The third is the recovering alcoholic and that's where I fit in. Many times, people have asked me, after being sober for so many years, why do I still go to meetings? I tell them it's because I still have the disease, which controls my reactions, which I'm powerless over, which is the same as a practicing alcoholic, and my reactions will end up controlling my actions which I'm not powerless over today. Then I would end up losing everything, as a nonpracticing alcoholic would do. Always keep in mind you do not have to drink to hit rock bottom. Rock bottom is a mental state, not a financial state. The alcoholic has a built-in attitude that constantly wants to hit rock bottom. With the drug and alcohol or without the drug and alcohol, the disease is not particular. I used to come to meetings because I was afraid of drinking and using again. Today I go to meetings because I am not drinking and using again. Before, meetings were for my addiction; today my meetings are for my attitude. My reactions are still powerless over the disease, rather I drink or not.

In working to restore my attitude, I take a walk with Grand Father Spirit and listen to the silence of the wind. Know that silence helps healing. If you listen, you'll hear answers as the teaching handed down from our ancestors say, "Silence speaks louder than words."

The Twelve Steps of recovery can be used for any issue in your troubled life, if you use them. Until then, the Twelve Steps are just words hanging on the wall, as words were when we were out there drink and using. How many times have you used the words, "I'm going to quit," while sitting in a bar or in jail somewhere? The result of not taking action on those four words is that nothing changed in your life, right? Now after years of saying those four little words, "I'm going to quit," you finally put them into action. Your whole world would start to change, making a 180-degree turn in your life, and you start seeing a whole new better life. Well, the Twelve Steps work the same way. Just keep in mind, if you are capable of putting four words in action with a wet brain (drinking), then you have what it takes to put the Twelve Steps into action with a dry brain (nondrinking). I personally used the Twelve Steps for more than my drinking career. I used it in a loss of a separating relationship. In addition, when I quit smoking some years ago, and of course for my drinking and using. In step one, it says, "We were powerless over . . ." You just put whatever word you want to work on in the place of alcohol, and go for it. When I have a problem, the first thing I do is rename the word *problem* to the word *tool*. Now I have something to work with. What say we take a walk side by side with the Twelve Steps and bring along the problem or *tool* as I mentioned? First of all, we have to know who were dealing with. So let's look into the mirror. Hey, what do you know? It's the same guy that was with you in all the bars you got drunk in; now you remember it was the same guy that keep you company while in jail for DUI. Matter of fact, it was all this guy's fault for all that other junk you had to go through just because this guy in the mirror could not say no to drugs and alcohol. So now we know we have an alcoholic looking back at us. This is called step one.

In meetings and the Big Book, we find a complete description of that guy in the mirror. Thanks to the description and examples from the Big Book, we're able to have a blueprint of this guy's life. Now as we look at our blueprint that we got from the Big Book, we see that we are going to need a carpenter since we don't have hammer and nails to reconstruct our house in the blueprint. We are convinced that only a good carpenter will be able to make the changes in our house. This is called step two.

Pay close attention here—there might be a test when I'm finished. You never know. Now let's get back to basics. Okay, now we go out in search of a carpenter that we can trust to do a good job. Lo and behold, someone in a meeting gave you a reference to one of your interest. So you go out by yourself and give this carpenter an interview, and by gosh you found one for the job. Now you turn the job over to him to reconstruct your house. This is called step three.

You and the carpenter take a walk together, before he starts the job, so you can explain to him in all honesty why the blueprints are the way they are. This is called step four.

Since you're spilling the beans anyway, you figure you might as well lay it all on the table. So you take the carpenter back a few blocks to step one where you admit to him why these blueprints you drew for your house are so messed up. This is called step five.

After you get that all off your chest, you relax and have a long, long conversation together and develop a strong, trusting bond between you two. Now you are convinced this is the one for the job. This is called step six.

Then you pick up the roll-up blueprints and hand them to the carpenter and ask him if he would take the job to help you rebuild your house. He takes the blueprints from you and says with a smile, "That's my job. I'll take it from here." That's called step seven.

Pen and paper in your hand, you look at the blueprints of your old house with the carpenter.

Then, as you look at the blueprints, you write down where you deliberately put walls up to annoy particular individuals. This is called step eight.

Now checking your list, you erase those walls from your blueprint except for the ones that will damage anything in your house. This is called step nine.

The carpenter will work on your house for a while then refer back to the blueprints. A little work on the house then back to the blueprints again to see what else needs working on. Trusting in him, you keep your alcoholic mouth of yours shut when he informs you what needs to be done and what he needs you to do to help him. Then make the corrections with him. This is called step ten. (Don't lag behind now; we're almost finished. Keep reading. Okay, here we go again.)

Now as he works on your house, you keep asking him if there anything you can do to help. If there is, you don't hesitate in doing so. This is called step eleven.

Now your house is looking good so you and your now best friend, the carpenter, go for a long walk together and you thank him for what a beautiful job he has done in your house. You let him know that you will forever be indebted to him and will refer him to anyone who seeks him. This is called step twelve.

The Twelve Steps is part of the program. This is why we work them the same way we do the program, from the inside out. I like to call this program a "me" program. We learn and recognize ourselves through others. This program is a perfect example of the saying, "I am the audience, and the world is the stage." Because that's exactly how this program works. You come in, pipe up, and watch your show. It's a way of letting the program come to you from the inside out. If you grab the program from the outside in, then once again you're doing things your way. And of course, when you do thing your way, you're taking things in your hands again. When you're taking your life in your hands, lo and behold, you're playing the power greater than yourself to yourself again. A bit of advice: just because you walk on water when you take a shower, it doesn't mean you the man.

When you take step one, you find, *self*, as I mentioned earlier, and when you do, you feel a hurt inside your gut. The hurt is because that's where you've been storing the hurt all these years. It's the same place you kept self for so long, deep inside. Just like a baby. When it's born, it has to be cleaned when it comes out. One has to clean away what the baby has lived in for nine months. If you don't clean the baby, the baby will die. The same thing happens when you take step one: the real you comes out, which is self. When it comes, out it's covered with hate, hurt, and all those other feelings you hid down there with self. Self has to be cleaned off just like the newborn baby. The baby you use a warm damp towel. Now self needs something different than a warm, damp towel. In this case, the Twelve Steps of recovery will clean off all the excess from self.

One has to learn to listen to self instead of yourself, meaning sooner or later you'll find that your insides know more of what you want and need than that noggin sitting on your shoulders does. Keep this in mind: the heart teaches the mind; the mind doesn't teach the heart.

You may be wondering what's with this inside stuff. Well, my friends, hang loose and keep reading. I'll explain. Okay, now listen up. When you first come into the program of Alcoholics Anonymous or Narcotics Anonymous, you have that big ball of hate, loneliness, hurt, loss, and abandonment deep inside your gut. If all that is deep in your gut, why would you go anywhere else on your body to fix it but inside? Think about it, and that's what we work on in the program: that which is inside you, not what's in front of you. Then too, think of it this way. If you have a problem with your foot, you go to a foot doctor. If you are having problems with your back, you go to a back doctor, and if you're having trouble with alcohol and drugs, you go to an NA or AA meeting. Why a meeting? You go to a doctor with your alcoholic/drug problem, he will understand. You see a psychiatrist, he will understand also. Everyone will understand, but you go to a meeting they will relate. The truth of the matter is that only a person with our disease can help another person with recovery. You have to be able to relate and know exactly where the pain and pressure are coming from and how it feels. This is what brings us together. I know there are a lot of nonalcoholic counselors out there that disagree with me on what I just said, but not one can relate to what I feel; they can only just imagine.

The individuals I just mentioned above are apt to give you suggestions through their authority in their profession. Then you end up being a puppet of suggestions. They will give you suggestions from the books they read in college. That's all fine and dandy, but keep this in mind. Every individual in AA, or NA from the year 1935 when AA had the name, "The squad of nameless drunks," to 1953 when Narcotics Anonymous was brought into the program, and up to today, our personal lives, wrote those books. We don't only read about the program; we work the program.

Recovery is not full of challenges but full of opportunity. There are no obligations in this program, only suggestions. All of the incidents that occur while in recovery happen so that we may learn and grow from them. As we may use them as tools of opportunity. Solving a problem is not as important as learning from it. Many times, one spends too much time looking at the problem and not seeing what he is to learn. Generally, the answer lies in the learning of the issue. Life is but a seed that's planted in us that grows when we nourish it with the power of wisdom, as in step twelve. Sobriety is a tool. We have to put it to work just like any other tool in order to get a job done, and the job is *our lives.* Speaking just for myself, I want more than just to get clean and sober and spend the rest of my life just sharing about it. I want to use what I have; sobriety to me is a hallway with many, many doors of opportunity. Behind each door is a new beginning of different ways of life that we may choose from to become whatever you want to be in sobriety. In sobriety, the reality of our dreams is right at the tips of our fingers. Everything we do in the program of recovery has its reality. You can go as far as you want in this program; the program only stops when you stop. One of my goals in recovery is to be better than I was when I started drinking and using. Without that, I would have been just sober at the same level of life from where I came from when I started drinking and using. One has to remember when we started drinking or using, whichever one, we stopped growing. That's what made us feel so different from the rest out there. The other world was getting somewhere and ours was not. So we got high and learned to fantasize on what we wanted to be so that we can feel part of. I myself practiced drugs and alcohol for twenty-three years, so that meant I had twenty-three years of growth to catch up on just to get the ball rolling. This is why I want to be at a higher level of life than I was when I started using drugs and alcohol. Besides that, it's a very dangerous place to be anyway. If I was happy there where I came from, then why did I start drinking and using?

Speaking just for myself, I wanted to get away from where I was because I was not good enough so I ran away from myself, and at the time, the easiest way I knew to be better was to fantasize through drugs and alcohol. I reached the point in my practicing of drugs and alcohol that I didn't care about reality anymore because I had gotten so used to living in my imagination. Many times, we just don't give ourselves a chance, but later in recovery we find out that we have always been the person we always wanted to be; we just told our self weren't. Knowing this, I have found contentment within myself where I no longer want what someone else has as I did when I first came into AA. I'm comfortable with what I have. This program eliminates the person you imitated when you were drinking and using and leaves you with that wonderful human being you left behind so many years ago.

Even so, we will still have our days when things start to go wrong. All the time, the solution is generally in the mirror that can be found in step four. Step four is to experience yourself and see where you're coming from. When I anticipate a bad day coming on, like things not working out for the day, I automatically turn off my expectation switch and just do what I like, and if I can't do what I like, I like what I do. In other words, "If all else fails, try appreciation," not the drug or alcohol. What we learn through this we would want to keep. We do this by giving it to someone else by sharing with others in meetings of recovery. Remember these meeting are rooms full of mirrors. In relating, we see ourselves and compare our issues with others. So when you share, become one of the listeners yourself so it will reflect back to you, or you will deprive yourself of your own message, which some day may save your own life. Never underestimate the power of your message.

Experience your personal powers. In other words, for example, my Native American brother gave me an eagle feather for spiritual, inner, and outer healing and strength. As I hold the feather in my hand, I think of how my ancestors believed in the eagle and how good it was that I can relate my spiritual growth with the wings of an eagle. In many ways, I can relate the eagle with the program of recovery. To begin with, the wings of an eagle are not strong enough to raise the heavy weight of the bird too high off the ground. The wings become to tired and powerless when it reaches a certain height. Just like when we become powerless when we reach our limit. But when the eagle's wings get tired, the eagle spreads his wings full length. As we reach out to any length to reach sobriety. The eagle lets the warm air and wind accumulate under its wing. The same way we humble ourselves by accumulating ourselves with knowledge and wisdom from meetings and sponsorship. Even though the wings of the eagle are tired and powerless, the warm air and wind will raise the bird even higher. As our spiritual body rises with dignity, with the warmth of love that we developed in our hearts through the program. As long as the eagle keeps its wings reaching out, accumulating warm air and wind under its wing, it will keep rising higher and higher. Same as we keep coming back. We get a higher conscious with our spiritual self. This is why even though the eagle has the weakest flying power of all other birds, it is still the highest-flying bird of all others. Once again, even though we are powerless over people, places, and things, we can still go high enough to go over them and continue flying as in step eleven in the Twelve Steps of recovery.

You can't argue about who you are, even though you may try, but you can change it. What I'm talking about is step one and the serenity prayer. "Accept the things we cannot change, and change the things I can." All the time I was out drinking and using, I only lived the first part of the serenity prayer. And in turn, I thought I was in the world I was put here for by accepting the things I cannot change, and that's it. But when I came into the program of recovery, it wasn't long before I learned through the people there that there was another part of life. "Change the things I can." I can change me.

I found that accepting the things I cannot change does not mean to marinade in your sorrows. You have to hang on to something in order to give it permission to hurt you. It's up to you what you want to dwell on. Nothing heals until the pain is gone because that's when you let go of it. We do not marinade ourselves in the things we cannot change. "Accept the things we cannot change." Accept: let's say the word. If you put dirt and water together, the dirt will wash away. This is what we do: wash it out of our lives. It's called turning it over. Then work on living life with a purpose as in step eleven.

This is what is called exercising our given personal power: make a decision and follow through with it. We have to recognize a power greater than yourself, as well as your own personal power without trying to take the place your conscience power greater than yourself. If you can say no to a drink and sit in a meeting instead, then you're exercising your personal powers. This proves that you have strong abilities. Recognize these potentials within yourself and give yourself credit for it. Remember it takes a power greater than yourself, and, I say again, your personal power too. It's like two to tango in this game. This is a way of developing responsibility. This is one of the first things an alcoholic loses in the world of crossfire. To create results in this program, we have to use our personal powers. First off, we have to identify *powerless*. Powerless lies in the diseases, and in the diseases is where the person we imitate lives and waits. Powerless over alcohol; powerless over people, places and things; and so on. Powerless does not mean helpless. Your personal reality is what you focus on. Let's focus on the word *were*, as in the Twelve Steps of Alcoholics Anonymous first step states. (We admitted we *were* powerless over alcohol.) This is a past-tense statement. Therefore, if you haven't had a drink today, then you have the power to say no to alcohol. As for myself, I was powerless over alcohol, but now I have the ability to say no. I am powerless over people, places, and things, but not the ability to turn them over. Let's not forget we may be powerless over some things, but never helpless. Whatever the mind is capable of putting in, the mind capable of putting out. This is what is called personal power. The only things I concern myself to other people's lives are my acceptance and my reactions. The state of your sobriety in the program determines your behavior and your reactions. Sometimes you are not responsible for your reactions or actions, but in this program, you are always responsible for your state of mind. Our minds have a tendency of overriding reality. I don't concern myself with what other people are going to do, only what I'm going to do, because that's what I personally have to live with. The program teaches me how not to anchor my serenity with people, places, or things, as in steps six and seven. First of all, they're not mine to deal with anyway. Step three doesn't have my name in it anywhere. That must mean he is; I ain't. When people, places, or things become obstacles, I take it of school so I can dissolve it into a learning formula and see what I can learn from it in order to get rid of it. That's what meetings are all about. Everyone has the ability to control and change their focus. Everyone in a meeting of Alcoholics

Anonymous is proof of that. Everything in these programs is constructed to help you straighten your personal power. To gain personal power, you first have to release yourself from all restrictions, such as hate and anger, and replace them with love and compassion, which is developed through the Twelve Steps of Alcoholics Anonymous. It all starts with you.

The program of recovery is a state of opportunity. In another way of putting it, the program is a force of direction in which *we* direct through acceptance. Acceptance by giving attitude permission to let a particular situation in. Every emotion has a force. Force is the behavior or life. Turn that force into a result. Our responsibility is to direct these forces in the direction of spiritual growth in our lives. We don't learn anything in life until we accept it first. As alcoholics, we run from it because of fear of pain. Everything we do in life is to avoid pain, even if it's just for the moment making it worse by thinking only of the moment in alcohol and drugs and not the results ahead of you. This is the way the disease communicates with you. Develop a caller ID within yourself so you know which opportunity is doing the calling. Have you ever heard "Listen to your first thought"? That's because the second one is generally the wrong number. Also, when in doubt, the answer is generally no.

No one here likes pain, failure of success, or rejection, which are sources of pain to all alcoholics. We try to avoid pain because we have the desire to gain pleasure. Therefore, when we fear failure or rejection in what we're trying to achieve, we turn to something else instead: procrastination. Procrastination through alcohol and drugs. It's a way to avoid pain. The two biggest forces of an alcoholic are pain and pleasure; the Twelve Steps teach us to control pain and pleasure. The need to avoid pain is a greater motivator than the desire for pleasure. Generally, the results of running from pain create a lot more pain than what you started off with. Whatever you don't correct today, you will have to repeat it tomorrow kind of situation. The thought of pain is an anchor. Therefore, focus only on the pleasures you'll have in success, not the pain or what you have to go through to get to success. Remember in this program we always keep our glass half-full, not half-empty. When I take each step, I always think of what I gain from it, not what I lost from it. In order to lose something, we end it because it's no longer there. But in the program of recovery, we have no *ends;* we only have new beginnings. The disease never dies. We just learn to use it as a tool to learn and grow from. One of the things the Twelve Steps tell me is that I no longer have problems; the Twelve Steps tell me today I have tools. It takes just as much effort to take the fork to the dark side of life than to take the fork to the bright side of life. The only difference is to take the dark side, you have to hold on, but to take the light side of life, you have to let go. It takes just as much energy one way or another. Just keep in mind that you live the results of your direction. Changing your direction of thought is all you're doing anyway; thoughts are energy. Let me put it another way. If your mind is able to put something in, then it's able to take it out. When you walk through the doors of a recovery meeting, you are in a different thought pattern, or you would have walked through the doors of a bar. Think of the results of not having that drink or drug, not what you have to go through not having that drink.

Some people come into the program and learn the Big Book of Alcoholics Anonymous and all the fine print by heart. But they seem to be at the same place they were when they started drinking and using. The only accomplishment they have to show in their sobriety is another day sober. Some people are content with the idea of being who they used to be before they were caught in the crossfire. When I had three or four years of sobriety, I myself hadn't accomplished a damn thing except for another day sober. I finally came to realize that sobriety is an open door to opportunities. One of the opportunities in this program is being able to turn your disease around and make it work for you instead of against you by changing the meaning of things that happened in your life. If the meaning doesn't change, then your life will stay the same no matter how long you stay in the program sober. Everyone is different in the time laps for setting a second goal in the program of recovery. Need I mention the goal in the program is staying sober to achieve serenity in our lives would be the first goal of all? Only when the individual feels comfortable is it time to make that move into a second goal in life. Remember you can't give what you don't have. What one needs is a positive, determined mind to achieve a goal that is developed through the Twelve Steps of Alcoholics Anonymous. The program offers a stronger conscious.

It is not in a safe field for an individual in recovery to start taking big steps in reaching a goal at first. Let's not forget that we came out of a very lazy mental state of mind, and our minds are not in shape to take on some heavy stuff right off the bat. This is where the exercise bit comes in. Just like we exercise our bodies, we exercise our minds. We feed our bodies for health and we feed our minds for health. Start off with small goals first and after a few accomplishments go to bigger ones, then bigger and bigger ones. At first, don't start off with goals that are going to rip your heart out if it's not accomplished. Get one that's within reaching distance. Remember, at first you're only exercising. Use the program to start off with; try to make so many meetings in so many days. If you say thirty meetings in thirty days and only make twenty-five, you have twenty-five meetings under your belt. Give yourself credit for what you completed anyway. No matter how small or how big your accomplishments are when you try, always give yourself full credit for it. Keep in mind that if an alcoholic doesn't get full of meetings, they get full of bull. Same thing with the Big Book. Commit yourself to one chapter a day and only read one-half of a chapter. Hey, at least you're in the right direction. No harm done with an exercise like this one. Just don't make things difficult for yourself.

I remember when I had difficulties I used to say to myself, "I'll be glad when this is over so I can go on with my life." Come to find out, later in time, that it was just the opposite. I had to go through it in order to get the issue over with. Life lingers until we learn from it. We have a tendency of anchoring ourselves in situations, especially the ones that are not good for us. Never underestimate this sadistic disease we have. It will always try to unbalance our lives in this manner. Let's not forget the way the disease communicates with us.

It's all about balance of the inner and outer spiritual self that the elderly taught you; balance is where it's all at anyway. You don't go to balance; balance comes to you. Balance is not something you work on. Balance is a result. Balance is what you find at the end of a quest. As in the Twelve Steps, one works their way through eleven steps for the results of the twelfth step. The twelfth step is the only step you don't work on. As for balance, if you try working on balance, then you're interfering with Father Spirit's direction for you. Like working on the twelfth step without the direction of other eleven steps, this is a waste of direction. You receive balance through wisdom, as you would a spiritual awakening through the eleven steps. Even though there are twelve, remember the twelfth step is the result of the eleven beforehand. You seek wisdom by listening and seeing from the heart, not your ears and eyes, as you would with the inside job of the Twelve Steps of recovery. In reaching balance, we do not imprison our self from life by segregating our self, because it's an acceptance of life. In reaching balance in life, do what you like. If you can't do what you like, then like what you do. The strength in your character will bring you serenity.

The methods through knowledge and wisdom are the balance I'm talking about. With wisdom and knowledge, one can find his or her balance of their inner and outer spiritual self. Some of us don't honestly know the difference between knowledge and wisdom. Some people think they're the same. Many of you on the reservation were taught at a very young age that knowledge is the teacher of the mind; this is what the body listens to. Wisdom is the teacher of the heart and soul; this is what the child within listens to. In the program, knowledge tells us *what* we are, whereas wisdom tells us *who* we are. In order to achieve these teachings in recovery, we have to refer to the Big Book and the Twelve Steps. The Big Book teaches us by identifying us to *what* we are by opening our minds to reality. Then there are the Twelve Steps that teach us *who* we are through spiritual direction. Okay, let's break this down where even I can understand it. The Big Book teaches the mind, and as they talk about in the Big Book, wherever the mind leads, the body will follow. On the other hand, there are the Twelve Steps that teach us how to find who we are through spiritual wisdom and truth. The only way to change is to find truth (step one). Without truth, there is no change; without truth, there is no destiny. This is what is meant by "honest program."

When I think of balance, I think of what makes balance in one's life, and the answer I find is the Father Spirit's will. The Creator's will is always something you fall into if you let it through trust. The Father Spirit doesn't make rock and expect it to float. In other words, the Father Spirit didn't make you and who you are just to have you be someone else. His will is for you, not the person you imitate. Father Spirit's will will never be one that would be a burden to you. We have been running from ourselves for such a long time that we forgot who we are. The Father Spirit's will is translated so that only the one we've been running from can understand it, not the person we pretend to be. In the program, we learn to stop running and identify ourselves by going to meetings and relating with others. Through this we find self, and through the Twelve Steps we find that self is the one that a power greater than you made to get a particular job done in his world. May you find his will now.

While we're at it, let's talk about this power greater than yourself stuff. When someone says the words *power greater than you,* the disease within you hears leadership over you. Therefore, we feel invaded, so now we become rebellious and the first thing we want to do is put up a defense and limitations. To begin with, from childhood days we learn of the Father Spirit, and of many other belief of other kinds of higher power, so we become agnostic. But since your world fell apart and went to hell, you put up a brick wall between you and this something that is supposed to love you out there somewhere. So now you look up to the sky and say, "It's all your fault, and I'm not going to believe in you anymore." Remember we came out of a codependency world and everything is the other guy's fault. That is until we latch on to step one. I ended up popping my own bubble. If this something out there doesn't exist, then who the heck am I talking to? This is the insanity of the drinking thinking. It's not that the Creator is after us or anything like that. We just have to realize that since the day of one's birth, one starts a quest. Today if you're in the program, even if it's your first day, then you're in the midst to your quest. I'm not going to say that Father Spirit works in mysterious ways, because there is nothing mysterious about the Creator. We just don't understand him sometimes.

Sure, everyone came in here with a shattered world behind them. But now you're put, for some reason, in this program so that you can put it back together again. The wonderful thing about it is that you can put it back together the way you want, not someone else. Not only that, you can build this new life as strong as you want, stronger than ever before. You can look at your past in a positive way. For instance, know that everything in this world, bad and good, is put here just for you. Your only job is to put it in its proper perspective so you can learn and grow from it. Our life is nourished through our works.

For example, having your kids taken away from you, or your wife or husband leaving you. Since we lost all of our values out there in the crossfire, we tend to take it a lot harder when we lose a person than when we lose a home or business. So let's say having your kids taken away from you, or your spouse leaving you. The tremendous pressure of pain from the anger and hurt is on you. Now let's make that work for you instead of against you. First of all, the pressure we're talking about is a force. Some people are forced into working late hours at work, or to go into deep depression, and some into drugs and alcohol like we did to get rid of the hurt. Now remember what we said earlier about having the power to change and focusing our thoughts. Remember also the forks in your paths of life. This is one of the places in our lives we can exercise that practice in order to make us a better person. So why not use it to force us into digging deeper into the truth about ourselves through the program? We have to direct this force; it will never stop until we get over our situation at hand. We don't want to get rid of it through drugs and alcohol, instead we want to keep it and let it force us farther into sobriety. It's a force. Use it, for crying out loud. When you first come into the program, you're powerless, not helpless. The anger part of it, use that part of it too. Use that energy of anger against anger. Remember what got you into this mess is having a relationship with drugs and alcohol. Use this anger to fight this disease that got you into this mess. It's amazing how a native reaction can benefit one in growth in this program. The angrier one gets, the more they strive. It's all in the matter of changing our direction of thought. Your happiness in life is through your direction of thought.

Everything in life has a reason for it, especially your past, which is the most powerful teacher you will ever have in your life. This is why we never want to shut the doors on it, because the past is also the best reference you'll ever have in your life. It's called taking the bad and turning it into something so positive it will save your life. I bet you're wondering, *Why do I have to go through so much hell just to learn one sentence in life?* Well, let's go with it this way: in order to learn to swim, you have to get your feet wet first. The water may be cold at first, but that's part of the process of learning to swim. As in life, we have to go through the uncomfortable part in order to reach our goals that are set for us from the day of our birth, like I mentioned before everyone is born with a goal set for us by the Creator. One has to jump into the cold water. The water is cold and no one is asking themselves if they did the right thing. As we jump into recovery afraid of what people might think of us, now we're wondering if we did the right thing. Now back to our swimmer, he starts splashing and swinging his arms all around, drinking half the pool water. Same as us when we come into the program splashing around in our denial, fluctuation, anxiety, and whatever else we have in our duffle bag, trying to find the truth. Back to the swimmer, the swimmer finally surrenders to the fact that there is only one way to kick and move your arms in order to keep your head above water, like when we take step two. Now let's get back to our belly full of water swimmer. Now the swimmer learns that if he keeps his arms active, he has a good chance of not going under. In the program, we learn the same thing. As long as we keep active, we also have a good chance of not going under.

There is no such thing as an alcoholic without heavy losses. So don't sit there thinking that you lost everything because someone upstairs or wherever pointed the finger at you. And also, there is no such thing as unique in this life of recovery. So no matter what happens to you out in the crossfire or in the program, you're not the only one. Another thing we have to keep in mind is that we drank and took drugs to be unique for so long that we still have that potential of trying to be unique.

Losses have to be in order to create your life. There are many unveiled reasons for losses. As in life, we have to lose some things in order to gain other things. One door has to shut for another to open type of thing. Sounds crazy, but it's true. Many times, we really don't lose what we think we lost. They're just taken out and bettered then give them back to us. Like an old car you might say that isn't running right, it loses its engine just for a while to get rebuilt, then when the engine is finished it's put back in the car. The car runs like a dream. There have been many homes and families put back together with a white picket fence, and all the trimmings after losing them, then given back. Everyone has a hard time with losses, but alcoholics are especially sensitive to any kind of loss and have a very difficult time dealing with it.

Instead of trying to get over the issue of loss, work on the issues relating to your discomfort in the loss. Find out exactly why you feel disturbed for losing what you did. For example, a man and woman lost a relationship. Is the man or woman hurt because the child within lost a playmate, or is it the fear of losing control over the other person? Jealousy that someone may take your place and you would feel like you would be sharing your dominating interest with another. Maybe possessiveness is in the line of fire. These are the issues we work on, not the loss itself. We don't work with what is in front of us, only what is inside of us. Another thing to remember as before: know what the Father Spirit's job is. And know what your job is. In this case, Father Spirit's job is in front of you and your job is inside you. We accept losses more so than the average person, because a loss is a change, our biggest enemy. When something is there one minute and gone the next, we notice the missing but not the difference. This is an alcoholic's definition of change. We have a tendency of concerning ourselves with what's taken out instead of what's being put in. When one door closes, then another must open and there's nothing we can do about it. We are so used to making a bad decision then getting high and making it good in your head. So you feel no loss or change in the issue. Therefore, we get used to not dealing with mach losses in our lives. Now because of this, when we come into sobriety, this becomes one of our weakest points, because we're not being able to replace loss with alcohol. We have to face the fact that it's not there anymore and we have to accept the things we cannot change. So we become the spoiled child who can't have the toy they want. Now they jump into anger. This is where the anger comes in; we'll talk about that later. But for now, let's try to understand that in the stages of recovery, there are reasons for all the feelings you're going through, and it's not really the people, places, or things we think it is. They trigger it; we learn to control it (reaction—action). Now more about losses. When we were out there drinking, we always compensated for the value of our losses through drinking. HALT: hungry, angry, lonely, tired. Here to an alcoholic, lonely is related to as a loss; something is missing. You can relate this to loss in a relationship with someone. There are three stages of a separation. First, there is anger, second there is hurt, and third there is lonely. Generally, a loss in a separation from a man and woman is beneficiary to one or the other party. Let's get into loss a little deeper, like you can't lose something you never had. People, places, and things—if you never had a relationship with them, then you never lose them. Never work on something that is not yours. For example, two people buy a lotto ticket and either number comes up. One is an alcoholic and the other is a normie. The alcoholic will say, "I lost." The normie will say, "I didn't win."

The pain you go through separating yourself from the alcohol is mainly up to you. It's all in how much you surrender and turn it over. Taking step one and two is the icebreaker. When you take one and two, the program becomes easier. When you surrender yourself and turn over the alcohol, you will have stripped yourself down to just the alcoholic and nothing else. Then the alcoholic (you) is the only one left to continue their journey to sobriety. In order to change your future, you have to change self first.

Have you ever wondered why it's so hard to surrender? The answer is pride. You come into the program just full of false pride and refuse to surrender because your pride is full of anger. In order to surrender, you have to give up something that gave you security in the past. Now surrendering into the unknown takes a lot of trust. This is where we activate step three. This is another reason why we go to meetings—to see proof of the power behind surrendering. Also limiting the weakness in surrendering. To begin with, surrender is what we unknowingly do on daily basis anyway. Everything we do in life is because we surrender to it. We surrender to drink or not to drink. We surrender to going to meetings instead of going to jail, and on having relationships and so on. The list is like a battery: it goes on, and on, and on. Surrendering is not a newcomer in our lives. We just don't recognize it whenever we make a choice for ourselves. Actually, we're self-consciously used to surrendering. Whenever you make a choice, you have to surrender to one or the other to make it happen. So therefore, let's talk about what we are really afraid of when we surrender. How about the choice of what we are surrendering to and all that we have to give up in order to completely surrender? As it is, we alcoholics hate change anyway.

As you work the program, the crave then becomes farther and farther apart. When you start taking your steps, you will find that your craves for drugs or alcohol will start coming in flashes. The crave will not last long when it comes in flashes. If you can just hold on until the crave leaves. This is where sponsorship comes in. Call someone, and it doesn't have to be an appointed individual. Anybody in the program will do. It's a choice of sponsorship. Sponsorship comes from anything that is related to a recovery program. Which includes meetings, Big Book, Twelve Steps, and the best of all, a conscious higher power of your understanding. A person with a program of recovery is never alone in sponsorship. Like I just said about the craves, these craves will become farther and farther apart as you work the program. The program becomes easier and easier as you make it part of your life, and your life part of it. This is what they mean when you hear, "It's hard, but it's simple."

I have an addictive disease, which means I am an addictive person. I don't get habits; I get addictions. We don't have habits long because they turn into an addiction soon after we get the habit. The difference between a habit and an addiction is a habit you break and an addiction you treat. I have an addictive disease, which means I can and will become addicted to anything I associate myself with. If you want to change the destiny of your life, change your association. Change your thoughts by changing your associations, and your destiny will follow. This is why I have to hang with the winners. Learn to recognize the winners. Keep in mind when you do, principles before personality. Seniority is definitely not one of the qualifications for someone to be a winner. In this program, it's not what you know but what you do. In this program, one can have twenty years sobriety and be nutty as a fruitcake, and still live on the grounds they came from. Keep this is mind: you make the money. The money does not make you and who you are. Because of our addicting disease, our association with negative people or issues is like a virus to an alcoholic. We tend to absorb negativity more so than the positive issues. Let's also not forget an alcoholic tends to look for comfort in an issue instead of release. They're so used to comfort through drinking instead of living life on life's terms Negative people or issues will trigger an agitating mind in us. An agitating mind from a practicing alcoholic does not see truth or reality. Your pattern of thinking is the key to sobriety. Everyone reacts according to their thinking pattern. What the alcoholic does is based on what they associate things with, their personal definition of them. Our minds are continuously agitating because one thought links to another in our minds. Whatever the direction of the first thought leads, whether it's a negative or positive thought, the related thought behind it will follow in the same direction. We'll discuss related thoughts later in the book. This is why we have to keep working on our attitude; our attitude is our first related thought. Our reactions will be triggered by past experiences or what someone told us through power of suggestion.

Every one of you came here to change your destiny. Your destiny is based on your daily behavior. Everything an alcoholic says or does is a cause for some kind of emotion, and for every emotion, there's an effect. Every effect has a result that creates a direction; every direction takes you to your destiny. Learning is not enough in this program. You have to put it into action. You have to be willing to give unconditionally of yourself to the Twelve Steps in reaching your destiny in sobriety. Keep yourself around the influences of your destiny, and sobriety. Like sticking with the winners. Reject the associations that are not within the boundaries of your destiny or sobriety. Your level of motivation is controlled by your associations. If you want to change the destiny of your life, change your association. Change your thoughts by changing your associations, and your destiny will follow. Know this: for an alcoholic, a simple change in their life makes many major things change simultaneously. Every single action you take has an effect on your life.

You must continue to condition yourself with your program on a daily basis no matter how much sobriety you have. In order to do this, you have to start with self. You'll find the description of self in the Big Book of Alcoholics Anonymous. First, you have to appreciate yourself more, and you will develop a different attitude that will give you a different meaning to everything you relate to. Then you will better understand that your pain and fears are not with people, places, or things but with your own belief of them. Don't express yourself with equal pain; learn to express yourself without the pain.

In order to get what we want out of this program, we first have to know what we want out of sobriety. When we want something, we're seeking a different feeling than we have now. You want something because of what it will give you to make you feel different than you presently feel. First, you have to focus your mind and thoughts on what you want. Let's not forget, as mentioned earlier, we are capable of changing our focus and thought patterns.

Control and direct the focus of your mind to what you pay attention to in meetings, what you see in others, and how you see it. Whenever people speak, they're giving a picture. See it. Words are pictures. See the quality of the message given. Once again, it's not what they say but what you hear that you go home with. Because of your past experiences, your mind has accumulated many inconspicuous answers that can be used for your future. Your past is your dictionary, so find wisdom and knowledge today that tomorrow will have a meaning. Your mind will give you answers according to your state of mind. Your mind will respond in the same significance as the question you ask it. Like the old saying goes, you ask a dumb question, you get a dumb answer. Continuously focusing your mind on the quality of the people you come in contact with will keep the state of your sobriety in an intellectual state, allowing your program to turn itself in a growing direction, which will fill you full of ideas to achieve your goals in recovery. Our minds are capable of having all the answers for our goals if we allow it to.

In sobriety, you are the only one that can change your own state of mind. You have to continuously exercise directing and conditioning your state of mind in order to keep your program strong. Your state of mind will evaluate the pleasures in life that you have in recovery, because the strength of your program in recovery determines your appreciation. The more you change about yourself, the more your thinking will follow to what direction you change it to.

Change the state of your program to be on the positive side of life with your body. Let your body show your mind how you want to feel. You want to be happy, then smile. You want to be strong, hold yourself up straight. Let your body communicate with your mind. Use body English to communicate with your mind the way you walk, sit, and talk. Talk with authority and direction; sit with pride and alertness. Smile. Use your face expressions to express yourself. Use your body movements to communicate with your mind that your mind will know in which direction to send your thoughts for a better life. By these exercises, your life will turn itself in a growing direction, which will fill you full of ideas to achieve your goals. You give your mind direction, and your mind will give you direction. In whatever direction you lead your mind will be the same direction your mind will lead you. In other words, the more achievements, the better and stronger ideas come from it.

This method will also help you to develop higher values in your life. Value comes out of our experiences in our ups and downs, through our lives.

Everything we do is from the result of our past. Our values are being affected all the time, especially when we were out there drinking and using. In sobriety, we can control the level of our values. The road to recovery can be very interesting if you have high values. What you are most concerned about in recovery is where you put your values. Wherever your values are is as far as you will go toward your goals. If your concern is in the pain you have to go through to achieve sobriety, then your values are in the thought of pain, and as soon as you feel pain, you will no longer proceed toward your goals because your values are in the way of your goals. If your main concern is in the challenge, then your values are in the challenge; the challenge will stop you. If your main concentration of your program is in success, then you will achieve success because that is where you put your values. You go as far as your values. Whatever is more important to you to stay away from, if it's pain, failure, or the thought of having a successful life in sobriety, is the distance you will travel. No matter what it is, whatever the highest interest you hold is as high as your values will be. You will always go toward your values; your values are like the power of suggestion.

The four directions in success are WANT, IDEA, PLAN, and CHALLENGE. In the center of these four directions is success itself. In other words, the way to success has four different stages. For instance, WANT. You have to want to get somewhere in your sobriety. IDEA: you need an idea of where you're going with your sobriety. PLAN: find a direction in your program to follow. CHALLENGE: be willing to go to any length to achieve your goal. SUCCESS: your final destination, your beautiful reward. If you dwell on, or concern your interest on, any of these steps, then your program will not go any higher. If you change your values, you change your destiny.

Our addictive mind evaluates everything before we do it and evaluates it according to our attitude. Your mind runs through these steps I just mentioned, and where it sees pain, failure, or rejection, our minds will hesitate. Our minds will seek results. If you go through these stages and if you don't give yourself a pleasurable reason to keep going, your program will stop growing. Our minds have to know that the rewards and pleasures of success are far better than the challenge. Know your values, and you know what your focused on.

My alcoholic mind will override reality more ways than one; it will cause my values to override my goals. Let me explain. A lot of times, we get so wrapped up in trying, that we pass up our goals without knowing it. Because their concentration is on trying, not success. Let's not forget we can only concentrate on one thing at a time. A continuing mind never stops for water or to take the fourth step. Just like a charging bull, he will have his head down looking at the ground instead of any obstacles that stand in his way as he charges toward his target. But the bull will invariably pass his target. Some people spend most of their time in sobriety trying to be successful in their life after unknowingly passing all their opportunity. They feel that the most important thing in the world is striving for serenity, instead of being there. Ever since you came into this program, we have learned that, in order to get anywhere in your life, you must be successful within yourself. Which is very true, but some people spend most of their sobriety listening to lectures about serenity, mediating, and reading and memorizing the Big Book. Working and working to achieve serenity. But not getting serenity. In most cases, they already have serenity but don't stop to feel or enjoy it. We have to stop trying once in a while to recondition our mind, body, and soul. This is where your serenity is at. There is a good reason for steps four and ten to be where they are placed in the Twelve Steps of Alcoholics Anonymous. We have to stop every so often and take inventory to see where our values are. Serene is in self, so by going back and reconditioning the mind, body, and soul is very important in your road to serenity. Serenity is a result and not a gift. You don't get serenity by staring at a wall or staring at the Big Book or the Twelve Steps. You have to read and work them first. Your mind is like the rest of your body. If you don't keep exercising it, it will get weak and lose focus. This is why we have the slogan, "Keep coming back." Remember the secret of success is consistency. See success in yourself first, because success will draw success. A strong state of mind will think success and ways to achieve it within ourselves. This is where the answers lies.

The same goes for answers as it does for success. Some of us search and search for answers and yet never find them. Some people get so tied up looking for answers, even pray and pray for answers, with no results. Remember earlier we were on the subject of what your job is and what his job is. Well, here we go again. Second verse, same as the first. It's not always the father Spirit's job to hand over answers when you already have them within you; it's your job to open that door. What I'm saying is we don't look for answers in the program of recovery; we look for doors to open. Answers are a spiritual release that is within us. We don't see answers for our recovery; we feel them. We work with the program and the answer will work with us. Answer is a seed planted inside us while we were experiencing life through drugs and/or alcohol. In this program, we water that seed so that answers can grow out of it.

You're never too old to change. If you're saying you are, then you're using an excuse. If you give any reason for not being able to do your program, you're giving an excuse. In recovery, excuse means you don't want to. For whatever reason you use, it's only an excuse not to challenge your obstacle you come across in sobriety. Instead of making excuses for not challenging your obstacle in your sobriety, start making excuses for tackling your challenges. Excuses are nothing but bonds and anchors in your life.

So if your addictive mind is capable of recognizing a message, then it's capable of analyzing it. Nothing goes into our minds without being analyzed first. Our brain likes to test the water before jumping in. Our mind does not pick up anything it does not understand. In other words, our mind does not pick up anything it's not ready for. Our minds will pick up certain thoughts and messages for a reason. So whatever you have upstairs, you're ready for or you would not have it up there. If your environment is in shambles, and you recognize it, it's because you're ready to work on it. Never forget any job in your sobriety always starts with you first.

If we relate fear and pain with challenge, then our minds will want to turn away from it, and then our program will stop from growing. In recovery, we have to be willing to experience pain as one of the stages in recovery. In recovery, we go *through* pain and do not stay in pain. Don't concentrate on the pain, only on the results of the passing pain. Turn the situation around. Think of the positive results you will have after you learn what you're supposed to learn from the pain. Remember we don't get out of anything until we learn from it. Keep in mind pain and fear are not results; they are only stages. Because of stages, we say, "This too shall pass." The results happen when it's over.

We have to convince our minds that the rewards of not having that drink or drug is much more rewarding than the rewards from escaping the fear of the challenge. Keep your mind on the rewards of success in sobriety then that of the challenge. Change your belief you had through negative experiences in the past of what a challenge is, and recondition your mind into a level of positive, successful thought patterns.

The past holds nothing in the way of your future; the past is only a reference. Accept it that way. Turn old experiences into a learning experience. No matter what your past holds, you are capable of managing your life from it, if you have the desire to give it permission to do so. Understand the powers of life. Your negative past has a lot of power for today's growth.

Use your emotions—bad and good—to help you reach for a better and stronger program, and make dreams come true by taking advantage of the opportunity in sobriety instead of just in meetings and not putting it to work in your life. Use negative emotions as a reason to go the other direction in life. Use it as pressure to get into a better state of mind. Learn to manage that pressure of emotions to your advantage. Understand that all emotional pressure is for your benefit and is to be used as pressure to push you into focusing yourself in a better state of mind. Emotions give us strength, understanding, and compassion. Negative emotion is nothing but a tool to better yourself. Without negative emotions, you have no drive to go the other way. It's your will to direct your emotions on such a manner that they will be to your advantage. Direction of emotion is the key. You need a reason to go on; negative emotions are giving you a reason to stay strong. We work with that kind of pressure every day, and most of us don't realize it. When we're hungry, our stomach feels very uncomfortable. We don't just sit there in agony. We use that discomfort to tell us our body needs nutrition. We use that pressure of discomfort to push us to eat. When we're in a situation where somebody breaks our heart or hurts us in some way, we feel hurt, negative emotions, and violated. We let that discomforting pressure push us away, focus our minds, and put ourselves in a different position where this will not happen again. This is how we can use negative emotions to benefit from. We talk a lot about sobriety, so let's break it down a little so we can have a better look at it. Sobriety is a personal spiritual matter within yourself. Sobriety is a spiritual road one takes in order to find the balance of their inner and outer spiritual self. Sobriety is your own personal road to your chosen destiny that starts off with your imagination. Imagination is where desire starts to form. Desire will inspire your motivation. A desire is what can be a start of a new beginning if we follow through with it. But worthless if no action is taken in the word *desire*. As in the saying, "desire to quit drinking." The same goes for the word *believe*, as in step two: "come to believe." This is also worthless when no action is taken. But when just a little action is applied to either of these words, they will become the most powerful words in your life. Alcoholics have more desires than the average person because of our weakness in our daydreaming. Don't misunderstand me. There is nothing wrong with daydreaming, as long as you keep in mind that daydreaming is only a pacifier. Through the years, we have become used to imagining our desires through alcohol. Today we have the desire to stop drinking. This time it's with action instead of that drink. Some very important words in recovery are *desire* and *believe*. Desire, a direction, and believe, a foundation. Everyone needs a direction, and a desire gives us that direction in life. We just have to move in that direction in order to activate it. This is what we are relating to when we say, "Go to any length." We go in that direction. This is where *believe* comes in. Believe in yourself, and believe in the power greater than yourself of your understanding to help get you there.

Know what you want out of sobriety, and believe in yourself that you can do it. If you know what you want, your motivation will be activated. Positive thinking is a cornerstone for your sobriety. Sobriety is something that you are not powerless over. You have full control over what direction it goes. This is why we need to exercise positive thinking. Whatever your thoughts are, sobriety will follow. Your direction of thoughts is the leader of your sobriety. Sobriety is what you desire in thought; it's the reality of your thought. The way you put thoughts in your mind, rather it be positive or negative, is the key. It's the way you evaluate everything; therefore, the strength of your sobriety is the results of your thoughts. For example, the opinion you have of yourself will affect all your decisions you make in sobriety. You are what you think.

This is why we have to think of ourselves as worthy. Realize that you deserve the program of recovery. You deserve a break and another chance in life like everyone else in the program of recovery. You deserve to be closer to your conscious higher power, and you do deserve a much better life, because you're worth it. Remember this: when you were born, you were everything good the Father Spirit, put on this earth, and now he is willing to give it all back to you. Take it!

Working on your thoughts to help you with a better life. First of all, try to find something positive in everything you associate with. This will motivate positive thinking and will create a stronger program because what you think is what you get. It's like project a thought, project a destiny. One of the first things we learn in recovery is that you can choose the way you think. Hang with the winners to help you control your thoughts.

We have read a lot about thought, what you think, and the direction you execute thought, into your program, rather it be positive or negative.

When I first came into the program of recovery, the hardest thing I encountered in this program was positive thinking. I can honestly say when I came into the program, positive thinking really wasn't my thing. But I was doing a lot of positive thinking and didn't know it. I went to meetings; that's positive. I related with other people that shared; that's positive thinking, because you have to be honest with yourself in order to relate. Honesty at any time is a positive state of mind. Even in my anger, I honestly admitted to myself that I wanted the kind of programs other people had. In order to want something, one has to see some kind of good in it; this is a way of positive thinking. I was trying to find ways to stop hurting. That's a positive state of mind. So you see just being who you are makes you a positive person. What I'm getting at is positive thinking comes naturally if you let it. Negative thinking is put there by force directed through our direction, and choices. These are forces of emotions. As I said earlier, we have the capability of directing this emotional pressure in a direction that we may learn and grow from them.

To develop a strong, positive program, start recognizing the positive reactions within your response on a daily basis. You will be surprised how much positive energy you put out to yourself even in anger. When you're angry at someone and you refuse to speak to them, believe it or not, that's a positive issue. You're stopping negative emotions from agitating and/or stopping someone from getting hurt. If you just look at every issue in your daily life, you will find that you have a good start for a positive life. The many things we do and say positive have to be recognized no matter how small it is. Appreciation of oneself is a new beginning into a positive program. Recognizing your capability of natural positive reaction within yourself will reveal to you proof of your potential for a strong, positive program. Negative thinking is a form of self-destruction, especially for the alcoholic. This is because whatever we think on expands. This is why we seem to have the tendency of making little problems into mentally big ones. For this reason, we have to be careful where we direct our thoughts. The appropriate direction would be from the problem to the solution, not deeper into the problem. Use your head. You already found the problem; now look for the solution. In whatever direction you direct your mind, it will magnify the issue rather in the problem or the solution. Whatever the case, as an alcoholic we will most definitely react to it.

Learn to communicate with yourself in a positive way by giving yourself credit where credit is due. Tell yourself you're a beautiful person, and you deserve all the positive things in life. In positive communication with oneself, know the fine line between confidence and conceit. Once again, keep your mind directed and focused at all times.

Now let's get down to the most important source in our positive programming. Program is a series of operations, such as behavior, activities, and attitude, that leads to sobriety. First of all, what is the most important source in our lives? For myself, it's communication, because even if I had a million dollars, it won't do me any good unless I communicate in order to put it to use. You can't even have a relationship with the Father Spirit, the creator, without communication. I first had to learn to listen to myself when I shared in the meetings. I needed to say and listen to myself when I said, "My name is Mickey, and I am an alcoholic," and listen to myself and be my own listener when I read the Twelve Steps one by one out loud.

Okay, so much for communication for now. Instead, let's bring up attitude. This is another important source of your program. The state of your attitude determines the level of your sobriety and what direction your program is going. Either you control your attitude or your attitude will control you. So many people have asked me how I was able to stay clean and sober for so long, and my answer to them is, "I didn't. Only a power greater than I can restore me to sanity." With this attitude, I have been able to achieve twenty-eight of the most wonderful years of my life. One of the most important workshops in recovery is attitude. The quality of our attitude is what determines how we look at things. The way we see things determines if it's going to help us or not, and how we accept it determines how much we're going to learn from it. Your attitude determines your acceptance of what you hear in meetings. Everything in your daily life is through your attitude to accept as a learning experience or a reminder. If we're capable of learning, then were capable of teaching. This is why we are told to carry the message.

Now let's put communication and attitude together. Everything you indulge in communicates with you one way or another, rather it be mentally or physically. Now the value of the communication you receive is based on the kind of attitude we have when we receive it. Attitude is an aura that we have around us at all times. The aura is our filter of life. When we have a good attitude, our aura is clean, and when we have a bad attitude, our aura is dirty. Okay now, let's put communication back in the picture. When we receive a form of communication, it has to travel from the sender to you. In order to reach you, the message has to pass through your aura. "Now here we go with the good stuff." If your attitude is good, then the message will go through a clean state of energy and clean itself with your positive aura. Rather it is a good or bad message, you will receive it in a good state of mind. But if your attitude is bad, then your aura is dirty, and any form of communication you receive will filter through a dirty aura of energy and become negatively dirty itself. And you will receive it in a negative manner, rather the message be a bad or a good one.

I came into recovery with major questions. First, who am I? Second, what am I here for? Third, what do I want out of life? It takes just a few minutes to answer these questions but half your life trying to find the answer. The answers to these questions direct your destiny. This is one of the reasons the program is directed toward your attitude and not the drug or alcohol. The program teaches us how to live without the drink, so that leaves only you all by your little lonesome with no excuses of being powerless. The first step pulls you away from all that. First step states we *were* powerless. Now you have the power to push it away and work on self. These questions—who and what—will be answered according to the state of your attitude. *Attitude directs direction.*

Attitude has more power than anything else in our sobriety. Attitude directs communication, which is the most important source in our program. But the meaning of the communication received by us can easily be deteriorated with a simple bad attitude. If there is something on your mind that's driving you toward a bad attitude. The thing to do is take the subject to another recovery in pain and help them by using your problem as an example. This type of Twelve Step is how you turn your problem into tools. If you can't find someone, then go to a meeting and use your problem as an example to teach others in recovery that problems like yours are not worth drinking and using over, and be that example for them. Finding a positive use for your problems is what makes it a tool. There are so many ways you can turn your problems into tools in recovery. If you put it out there where you or someone else can learn something from it, then it's a tool. All you have to do is accept the fact that a problem is only a learning situation, and the only way out is to learn what you're supposed to learn from it, because then and only then will you know how to solve the problem. In all negative situations, a tool is your best friend in recovery. This is why we must turn all negative issues into teachers for yourself and others to learn and grow from. Remember what we said earlier: we are capable of directing and focusing our direction of thoughts. Since our minds can only focus on one thought at a time, and you are the director, then direct your problems to how you can help yourself and someone in recovery with it. You are capable of doing this if you're in the program. Take it from step one. "You *were* powerless." Now you have no excuse for not practicing this exercise.

Life is the accumulation of truth, and the truth is you're a beautiful person and there isn't a damn thing you can do about it. You can try to conceal it, cover it, camouflage it behind drugs and alcohol, but you will never change who you really are. See who you really are and see the quality of self so you will develop a reason to better yourself in life. Loving yourself is as important as loving others. The more your ability to love increases, the more your ability to be loved increases.

In the program of recovery, a healthy relationship is just as important as a healthy diet. Let's not confuse this relationship with something that is going to get you in trouble. The relationship I'm referring to is the relationship within. There are many kinds of relationships, but there is only one meaning to the word *connection*. There are many other relationships man and woman can have other than within themselves, more so a woman than that of a man. A woman is a lot different from a man in accepting relationships. A woman has a relationship with everything she is involved with. A man conquers everything he is involved in. Here is an example of what I'm talking about. A woman goes to the store to buy coffee. As she walks into the store, she starts looking at the specials they have, comparing prices from what she seen at other stores and so on. She gets the coffee and window-shops on her way out, developing a relation with her shopping. A man? Forget it. in the store, straight to the coffee, pay for it, history. He conquered his mission. Now back to the program with this relationship stuff. In the program of recovery, we have to build a relationship with ourselves. If you notice, I said *self* with an *s* at the end of the word (plural), which means there are two people here. Now you wonder who they are. Well, I'm here to tell you it's you and that little child you have locked up inside of you. Everyone—men and women—has a child within. I say child because this person inside you stops growing when your reason for drinking developed. Let's see if we can identify the child within. When you frown, the child is the one who cries; when you smile, the child is the one that laughs. This is the one you put in that dark place deep inside of you. Why do we do this to ourselves? As for the man, his reason is because he wanted to conceal his weakness. For a woman, it was for protection of her child. Now we know who they're talking about when someone mentions relationship with ourselves. Get to know this child within and know your weakness. Let that child know that it's okay to cry. let that child be your prayer behind your smile. Let that child be your best friend so that the child will know that it does not need a validation of a motherly image, or a man and woman relationship, to come out. Let that child know that you will be the one who will protect him of her. Eliminate validation for that child to come out so that you can feel your own presence when you're alone. No matter what you did to that child, that child will always come to you; that child is your unconditional love. This is called having boundaries for yourself. Let that child become part of you and you part of him or her. Learn to love that child. This is loving yourself, and what I mean when I say I am my own best friend. This is what makes you a whole person within. Giving yourself this kind of relationship will enable you to master all your goals in sobriety. Learning to love yourself is what sets you free and allows you to be happy for no reason.

When coming into the program, we are full of denial. Many of us come into the program and actually without realizing it look for denial. As soon as our personal defense comes up, so does our denial. Let's not forget alcoholics are so afraid of what people might think about them and validate themselves according to other people's opinion of us. Some might think we're breaking weak for coming into recovery; others might think we're stupid because we just come off the streets. Whatever the case may be, our guards are up. No matter what the reason is for these defects, we are capable of revealing that reason and using it as a reference in your program. This is one of the ways to turn your defects into a tool that you may grow from. Your defects are part of what you are, and there is nothing you can do about it but to change the direction of them, making bad guys into good guys by changing these defects of character to a positive source. Your defect is to escape reality. Give yourself a good reason to change directions of your defects from your character. Your defects are anchored down by your emotions. This is one of the reasons why one has to learn to be thankful for their opportunity from the reference from their defects. Remember everything—bad and good—that is put in your path is put there because you're loved and wants you to grow. Your only job is to learn and grow from it. Once you have learned and grown from a situation, you'll have a different outlook toward the situation. Then one can accept it altogether in a different manner. When one is thankful for something, it becomes a growth, and your emotion tells your thoughts which way to go from there. Your emotions are separated in two directions: hate and love. Now this has everything to do with changing directions of all these defects of character from one state to another, because if you're in the love state, then you will turn your character against the hate state. If you're in the hate state, you will turn your character against the love state. Every time things don't go right, your character would be to go out and drink and run from it. Now you have to turn your defects against recovery and using the energy of your defects to make things worse. On the other hand, if things don't go right and you work in the other direction toward the program of recovery to work through it, then you have turn your defect into a reference against alcohol and use your defects as a tool. Your defect is to escape reality, and you did that with the alcohol. Now use your defect as a teacher to bring you back to reality. remember the past is a lesson taught.

Denial is another defect of character that we can turn into a tool to help us. Let's look at it this way: this is recovery, not Joe's Bar. You don't have to be one step ahead of anyone artificially or otherwise. Keep in mind that this is a self-program. Denial is acting and this is recovery, not Hollywood. In recovery, denial is the characteristic of a practicing alcoholic. This is why it's very critical to work on your denial. Remember without truth there is no change. How many years have you sat at Joe's Bar convincing everyone that you have been around the world once and talked to everybody twice and this is why you're so smart? Then come into recovery not knowing anything? No way! So what we read the Big Book, take the Twelve Steps, get some sponsorship, go to meetings, and tell everyone how much your life has changed since you quit drinking. now on day two, you tell everyone, "You see, I'm cool with it." Don't laugh; we were serious.

Okay now, what is denial? Denial is a false representative of the true you. Let's turn denial around and make your characteristic of denial work for you instead of against you. Denial is a cover-up through imitating what you seek in life. There are many, many issues in your life that you can be in denial of. Only you know the truth. First off, find out what you're in denial of. This is your direction. as we said earlier, we need a direction. Get whatever you're in denial of and see it at a 180-degree angle. This is making it positive. For instance, if it's denial because of failure, see yourself in success, or shame see yourself in proud, or who you are. see yourself in pride, and so on.

Okay now, we have a heck of a good start. We have a direction and a goal. Our direction is the opposite of what we're in denial of. What we're doing here is making denial into a tool that we can use to help us grow in sobriety by making it a reference, and our goal is to achieve change. Whatever the target is, believe that there is no reason in the world you can't turn yourself into reality. Let's look at denial as a tool. Whatever you're in denial of is like water behind a dam. The water represents what you're in denial of. The dam represents denial. The first step in working on denial is denial itself. In order for the water to pass through the dam, we have to open a valve to let out the water so we can put it to use. So in our denial, we have to open doors so we can put what is behind them to use. As water flows through the valves that we opened, we're able to put it to use in watering the seeds we planted. The same happens when we open doors. we let out a flow of energy that can water the seed within us by using the reference that your denial has to offer you, and once again *our past is our directory.*

Believe in yourself and trust that there is nothing within you that you can't change. If you are capable of changing in one direction, then you are capable of changing the other direction. We fell into denial because drugs and alcohol convinced us that we are not what we want to be. The thing is we already are everything we ever wanted to be. We just have to learn to give it permission to come out. Never be ashamed of who you really are. The creator doesn't make junk; we do.

Recognizing our *needs* and *wants*, because of our alcoholic characteristic of selfishness, we always wanted everything. Wanted a drink, wanted love, wanted a woman/man, and so on. many of us never admitted that they needed anything. Coming into the program of recovery, we learn the importance between our wants and needs. In doing so, sometimes our little minds get kind of confused on our wants and needs. Since our alcoholic mind has a tendency of always taking the easy way out, this is why we must have a deeper feeling for need than we do for want. When we crave alcohol, or anything else, our mind registers: do I really need this or that? Because the alcoholic mind finds less constructional emotion in the word *want*, then the question is this: do I need this? The question in the word *want* generally falls into daydreaming, the no-effort way of life. There is no constructive responsibility in the word *want*, but there is in the word *need*, a word that has to be activated. When the mind hears the word *need*, it hears emotional responsibility. Need is mandatory; mandatory sees responsibility. Therefore, it's much easier to accept wanting something than to need it. "When our needs become our wants, we then live in appreciation. Then will there be serenity."

Early in my sobriety, I remember sitting in a meeting and hearing one person with some years under his belt say that we have to do the footwork. Then on the other side of the room, I heard sharing about letting go. In the meantime, I'm picking up two messages. one tells me that I do some footwork on it and the other tells me to sit tight and give it to Father Spirit. It's like one telling me to get up and the other telling me, "Don't move." It took me a while to figure out that there is only one message here: "Surrender." That is the footwork. The word *surrender* for us does not mean throw down arms as it states in the Webster's dictionary. We don't throw down anything; we strengthen ourselves by turning it over then using it to grow with. Just like taking your car to a mechanic for a tune-up so we can get somewhere with it. The word *surrender* in recovery means open doors and turning it over. Turning it over means take it out and give it to a power greater than yourself to fix. This is doing the footwork and letting go. Our job is to open doors. The more we open doors, the stronger we become. What is opening door? Being honest with self. It may be hard, but remember you're giving it to someone that already knows the truth. Opening doors is like taking a penicillin shot. It hurts when the needle goes in, but the results are well worth it. When we turn it over, we are making more room for self. To be self is from the inside. Being self means having your own heart. Never be ashamed of who you are.

In surrendering, it's like everything else in one's life. it all starts with you. You have to motivate surrender. One does this with a spark called trust. Trust is like a kickstand for surrender. Let's not confuse trust with expectations. Expectation is manmade; trust is spiritually made. Just believe in your trust and do not expect in your trust. Trust is a belief into another belief or faith into belief. If you find it hard to trust in order to surrender, then just like anything else that you find difficult to accept in the program of recovery, find something positive about it. See for yourself the result of others in the program of recovery who trusted and surrendered. The positive side is in the results. You will always find a positive result to every link in recovery.

We love to blow issues out of proportion and letting ourselves get all worked up while our brain gets all wacko. Lots of us find this exciting. This is what happens when we try to explain an issue that made us angry. We have the tendency of developing the snowball effect of the issue and following right behind it with anger. Feels good, huh? Anger is one of the pacifiers, a "quick fix" for us. Anything that encourages our adrenalin, we generally classify as a high. For example, anger, lots of coffee, sugar; some even use hunger. hunger makes you weak and dizzy. Get hungry and drink lots of coffee, which leads to anger. This is called setting yourself up. Your reaction is the disease; you will have feeling you're human; your action is the snowball effect of your feelings. As you blow your anger out of proportion, you start to feel good inside as you would a high. At the peak of your anger, the reason for your anger is no longer the issue. Your hundred-mile-an-hour adrenalin is. This only exacerbates the issue into more than what you started off with. As an alcoholic, we're apt to believe this magnified issue we created. And in this program, you are responsible for fixing your own feeling.

Anger also strongly affects your spiritual life. Profanity nourishes anger, (sets you up). Notice an individual who uses heavy profanity, and compare their way of managing anger with someone who doesn't use profanity. Changing the way you express yourself helps the growth in your recovery. I am definitely not saying without profanity there is no anger; anger is a human emotion. The point we're trying to stress here is that without profanity, we have better management with anger. Try keeping your mind in a positive state, because where you bring the mind, the body will follow. This relates to our reactions and our action. Reaction is the mind's normal emotion. Action is the body following. The way we set ourselves up for anger is the way we will respond to anger. Anger is not something that comes along and takes over. Anger is something that comes along and looks for permission to take over. In order for anger to overpower your actions, you have to give it permission to. As we said before, this disease comes from a codependent family in which we can identify anger as an emotion that occupies us while we try to control the issue that we are powerless over. I have shared in meetings many times that thoughts have energy, meaning today's thoughts are tomorrow's destiny. Anger is a good example of what I'm talking about. If your thoughts are negative today, then your thoughts will be anger tomorrow. Anger is a normal emotional reaction but can be a setup for your actions. We are the ones who set ourselves up for our actions to anger. Believe it or not, anger is like a rattlesnake: it never strikes without warning first. We just have to know the warning before anger strikes. You lose your temper because you didn't listen to your warning system. We have one of the best warning systems compared with people who don't drink or use, and it's called reaction. Why? Cause we're sensitive, so there we go again using our weakness as a tool to help us. Reaction works like your brain when it tells you to fix something on your body or it will be in great danger. Your reaction is telling you that your actions can be in great danger. Reaction is a warning system for you. Reaction is from human nature, and action is from you. Anger never comes in without checking with reactions first.

In the program of recovery, we learn to deal with our reactions before they turn into actions. How? With the Twelve Steps of recovery. The first step starts off by pointing the finger directly to you by saying, "We were powerless," which eliminates our excuse. As we would say, "I did it because I'm an alcoholic." No longer being powerless, as said in step one: alcohol is no longer the issue. We are. Because as step one commences to say, "Our lives have become unmanageable." Which directs the issue toward our attitude. From then on, every other step is directed toward our attitude, not anything we consume. Through this process of elimination, you know what you have to work on: just you and not the alcohol. In order to take the Twelve Steps of recovery, you have to identify each step in order to understand it better. How? We call it the Twelve Step Book, which identifies each step so that we know exactly what we're dealing with. This makes the Twelve Steps so much easier to understand and work with. Of course, keeping in mind that the more you understand something, the easier it is to accept.

When I relapsed and then came back to try again, I tried to figure out why I relapsed. Was it because I didn't go to meetings? But I did. Was it because I didn't work on the Twelve Steps enough? But I did look at the Twelve Steps. In this program, I have learned to work on my attitude, learning to live without that drink. Because, like I just said, the first step takes out alcohol and continues with the footwork on attitude, leaving out the alcohol to work with. now I have only my spiritual belief. Keep in mind when you separate yourself from alcohol, you're afraid of losing your security, so you become defensive, and this affects your ability to surrender. In the program, one will go to meetings, talk with sponsorship, work on the Twelve Steps of recovery, and so on. But you keep wanting to back out even though we know what it will lead to if we do back out. Then we wonder how we can want something so bad when we know it will surely kill us. Well, let's investigate. The relationship between you and alcohol can be related to a relationship of a man and a woman. Remember we were married to alcohol. Okay, let's compare these two, but first let's keep in mind that there are two parts of any separation. When man and woman go together for a while, they act like kids together. When I drank for a while, I started playing head games with myself and acting like a foolish little kid when I got high. Now when man and woman separate, even though the love is gone, there is something trying to pull them back together. As for myself, when I separated myself from drugs and alcohol, there was something trying to pull me back out again, even though I knew that kind of life would kill me. This is because I only worked on one part of the disease, the adult part. As we only worked on one part of the separation, the addiction part, we have to work on the separation of the child within also, because the child was involved in the relationship. Remember the child within always plays a part in any type of relationship you may have and never is eliminated from a separation. Same as alcohol taken away and followed by footwork on attitude.

In no way is the disease eliminated from our lives. We still have the disease part to work with. The two parts of man and woman separating are the adult and the child within. As we have the two parts of recovery of the alcohol and the disease itself. The child within reacts to your thinking. Always keep in mind, "Your belief is your reality." Separating from alcohol is a miracle from Father Spirit. Keeping it that way is a result from the program within yourself, and this is where you direct your concentration. The spiritual relationship you have between you and your conscious power greater than yourself is the distance between you and drugs and alcohol. The relationship you have with you and your spiritual self is the relationship you will have with the program of recovery. Your not drinking is a miracle from the Father Spirit; your attitude is a result of your chosen program of recovery. By working on recovering from alcohol, you work on recovering your attitude.

I have seen people who have ten, maybe fifteen, years in the program and start drinking and using again. Even though they swear up and down that they don't crave alcohol anymore, and truthfully, they don't. The craves are like waves in the ocean: they come in real hard then just slip away. Most people have fewer and farther apart waves of craving alcohol after some time in the program of recovery;

everyone is different in time lapse. Stopping alcohol is not like when one stops smoking. Even though one uses the same Twelve Steps we use for drugs and alcohol to quit smoking. I stop smoking eight years ago by using the Twelve Steps of Alcoholic Anonymous. It's the crave of the alcoholic thinking that gets you in trouble. Every thought is related to what is called a thought link. In other words, one thought always leads to another thought that's greater than the first thought in everything we say or do. Our related thought will encourage our first thought, or it will deny our first thought. This is according to our attitude. So even though there is no crave for alcohol, you're thinking and reacting like an alcoholic. Your direction of thought will lead you to using drugs and alcohol again. Once again, where the mind goes, the body will follow.

A lot of people are always trying to play tricks on reality with their mind by saying to themselves, "Maybe if I think this, then that will happen." Or you say to yourself, "When I think positive, then something negative always happens, so I think of something negative so something positive will happen." A lot of us develop a superstitious thought pattern without realizing it. We have the tendency of trying to situate ideas in our heads, trying to manipulate reality with our minds, and it's all behind us wanting to fix it ourselves and others. The alcoholic mind always insists on shifting thoughts around in our heads in order to fix them. This is what we call "trying to fix fixed." Instead of turning it over. Also, this is the type of crave we're talking about earlier, of trying to fix everything. This is what people are talking about when they mention "playing head games." Know the difference between the practicing alcoholic's thinking and the recovering alcoholic's thinking. The practicing alcoholic's thinking is their reality, and the recovering alcoholic's belief is their reality.

Theirs is no reason for going back out drinking again, but there is a result that leads to going back out and drinking again. The results are in the thinking that leads to drinking or using: where the mind goes, the body will follow. Everything in life is from a result. From a prayer in a result to a miracle, and from anger in result to your fate. The program is no different. Results are created, not handed down. In prayer, you don't just pray. you believe in your prayer. In the Twelve Steps, one doesn't just take the Twelve Steps. One works the Twelve Steps. In the program of recovery, you don't just come into the program ("Here I am" attitude). you create results from the program. As a newcomer in the program, I took the Twelve Steps by reading them over and over and never caught the punch line until one day I got personal with them. In other words, I took each word from the inside. I took it as if each word belonged to me. for example, in step one, "We admitted we were powerless over alcohol." The word "We" tells me there are others who relate with me. "Admitted" tells me that I must have the courage to be honest with myself. "We" tells me I'm not alone. The word "were" tells me I have a chance to make the alcohol a past tense. "Powerless" tells me to let go and let a power greater than myself take over. and "over" to me means "finished." "Alcohol," of course, tells me where the problem is with me, and so on. By taking each individual word and identifying with it, you become part of it. Isn't that what we've been looking for all along, "being part of"? It's the same with the program. learn to make it part of you also. You work the program to create a program as a result by letting yourself feel what is said in meetings. Listen to what is said in meetings as you were in the movies, and you're the star. In other words, listen with the mind's eye picture yourself in what people say in meetings. This is how you relate.

When we become part of the program, and the program becomes part of us, we achieve courage to tackle the goals we always dreamed about. So now with self-confidence, we start our journey to one of our many goals. At the end of one of our goals, we have wisdom, growth, and rewards. What's at the end of each journey belongs to you. what was in your journey to your goal belongs to your brothers and sisters in recovery. This is why we have meetings so we can share our experience, strength, and hope. The knowledge and wisdom we find in our journey, we share in the meetings. Knowledge teaches the mind; wisdom teaches the heart. Remember in recovery we heal the body and mind. To keep your knowledge and wisdom is to be a teacher of it. This is when the student becomes the teacher. Become one of the listeners yourself when you share, and you will have learned what you taught. then it's yours. You have given it away in order to keep it.

It is said that you can't change what is written. I personally agree. It is written who you are; therefore, that's who you'll always be. Now let's take note and pay close attention to this. What was written was written in two books. This includes your defects and everything else in your life. What I'm saying is that there are two directions for everyone to choose from. A book is written for each of these directions. For example, it is written in one book that you make a decision to stick your hand in a fire, you are going to suffer the consequences. and it is written what you are going to go through as a result. In the other book, it is written that if you walk away from the danger of the fire, there will be no pain or danger as a result. It is written that you will go out drink and use then live a very, very hard life and suffer the consequences as a result. On the other hand, in the other book, it is written that you didn't take that drink or use, and in not doing so reached many, many goals in sobriety and lived a good positive life as a result. It is written that you let your defects get anchored down by your emotions and you and your love ones suffered the consequences as a result. In the second book, it is written that you work on your defects of character and direct your defects into a 180-degree turn into a tool pattern and achieved a growing positive attitude as a result. Your destination is already written; it's up to you which book you choose to read. The moral to all this is that if you drink and use, you only have but one way to go . . . *For it is written!*

Let's talk about letting go for a while, okay? For us, not letting go is a control issue of safekeeping. Many of us don't let go because not letting go gives us a chance to exercise our fantasy world that we have so long grown fond of that made us feel like we had full control over. As long as we predict, then we feel we're in control of it. If we let go, we no longer have toys in our heads to play self-destructive head games anymore. Developing fantasies in our heads is one of our greatest past times. This is why we say, "An idle mind is a dangerous mind."

Letting go can be very difficult yet such a small sacrifice for a healthy life. Sometimes people don't let go because it brings them the attention they crave. I have known some people that refuse to let go of a death because a loss of a loved one brings them sympathy. Other times, one doesn't let go because it gives them a reason to feel sorry for themselves. The alcoholic mind will always, and I mean *always*, find a reason to stay away from self. This is only one of the reasons why we have to continuously work the program.

Personally, when I came into the program, I figured as long as I had it in my head, it would always turn out in my favor and let my fantasies become my reality. As long as I don't let go, I will be close to it, and letting it go is taking a chance of losing what little I have left of it forever. Then on the other hand, we may be afraid of losing it, so we leave a little spark behind, which one calls not giving up. I used to think that not letting go is holding on to hope, but I was going through hell with it. If that's the way to have hope, then why in the world did I get so messed up with it in the first place?

Material things and issues are not where we put hope, faith, or trust. Try your conscious spiritual belief instead and let it recondition it for you and give it back to you. Let's call "letting go" "recycling" it. See through others such results of letting go. The closer you get to your conscious spiritual belief, the more strength you have to let go. Without a conscious spiritual belief, you have no strength. The saying, "This too shall pass," is very true if you walk away from it. When you do realize that your control is only a mental state of mind and you turn it over to the Father Spirit, be sure to put something positive in its place. Remember the human mind can only think of one thing at a time. As we mentioned before, every thought has a related thought. Let's not forget, the alcoholic's mind is always hungry. So whatever you put in your head to replace what you let go of will grow. this is why we keep our thoughts positive by having faith. In the meantime, work on growth. whatever you turned over will be healing also. life just works that way. So whatever you let go of heals. you'll be humble enough for it, if you so desire to accept it in your life.

As I said before, every road has two directions. either we can travel into the spirit of darkness or the other direction that's into the spirit of the light. If your heart is capable of leading you one way, then the same heart is capable of taking you the other way. In other words, if the heart is capable of putting something in, then it's capable of taking it out. So if you have the strength to pull one way in your life, then you have the strength to pull the other way. To believe in yourself is the strength, to surrender is the strength, and your willpower is the strength. Know that the medicine in willpower is the miracle. This disease is not like any other habit you had to stop because it's not a habit; it's a disease. A habit takes willpower. This disease takes a miracle. This is why we must have spiritual strength and a strong belief within us. Know the balance between willpower and miracle. The willpower to say no is the miracle to another day sober. the willpower not to pick up that drink is the miracle of another day sober. the willpower not to have that first drink is . . . You guessed it.

I leave you with this: Know your enemy. People, places, and things are not the enemy. Hate is what we call the enemy. Man fights man, or brothers and sisters, and not the enemy. Only in our vision of people, places, and things do we see the enemy lie. Know that only the Great Spirit can fight the enemy, rather it's in the inside or the outside of us. Hate, the enemy, is only within you. Our hearts are the givers of hate; our hearts give birth to the enemy, if we allow it to . . .

Au-ho.

www.ingramcontent.com/pod-product-compliance
Lightning Source LLC
Chambersburg PA
CBHW030402290526
45785CB00004B/1867